The Error Free Workplace

How to Write Work Instructions

that

People Actually Want to Read

ISBN-13: 978-0692123294

First Edition

The Error Free Workplace

How to Write Work Instructions that People Actually Want to Read

by Kyle Shropshire

If there's a button, it's meant to be pressed.

-Kyle Shropshire

Table of Contents

List of Figures

List of Tables

Introduction

Welcome to "The Error Free Workplace." This book will teach you how to create work instructions that people actually want to read.

Most technical writers do not devote enough time or effort to create acceptable work instructions, and their hastily written work instructions fail to reach full potential and lead to reader error.

Writers who take the time to craft the best work instructions increase reader productivity and reduce errors. Their instructions eliminate error because clear and helpful information is presented to readers. The readers are able to focus on the task at hand rather than trying to decipher what the instructions mean.

Figure 1: Learning process vs. Deciphering instructions

When readers know that your instructions contain clear and helpful information they will be more likely to read through the document and follow the directions. The main goal of this book is to help you create these types of user-friendly work instructions.

By the end of this book you will gain the following abilities:

- Understand why most work instructions fail.

- Build a framework that allows the quick creation of familiar feeling instructions.

- Create a style guide to keep documents consistent.

- Write concise steps that convey all necessary information.

- Place and format images appropriately for technical documentation.

- Apply helpful tips that I have gathered from writing my own work instructions in a manufacturing environment.

These topics will help you build a solid foundation and get you started on the way to writing work instructions that people actually want to read.

Applying the Concepts

As you progress through the book, I encourage you to work on your own version of the documents that are presented. This will allow you to get valuable hands-on experience with the topics as they are introduced. Another benefit to this approach is that by the end of the book, you will be able to immediately use your documents to create work instructions. These documents will provide a solid foundation that can be updated as you gain more experience and receive feedback from your audience.

If you choose not to work on your own documents, an example is provided at the end of each relevant section for you to review.

So, let's get started.

Chapter 1: The Problem

An effective, well-written work instruction leads inexperienced readers through a process without confusion. Unfortunately, finding a great work instruction is rare. Try to think of the last time you read through a set of instructions and did not have any questions or doubts. I would be surprised if you can think of more than a couple that meet these criteria. Most instructions fail for one of the following reasons:

Spelling Mistakes

Spelling mistakes are one of the most common issues that plague work instructions. Misspelled words somehow persist, even though spell check features are present in most software. Errors of this type are generally harmless because the reader is still able to complete the process.

However, this type of simple mistake lowers the reader's overall opinion of the instructions and of the persons who approved them. This is especially true when the instructions are read by people outside of the company. Work instructions are some readers first impression of you and your company, and it would be unwise to appear subpar due to simple mistakes, as this may cause new readers to view you, or your company, as unprofessional. They will question the accuracy and safety of the instructions, thinking that the writer did not even take time to correct simple mistakes.

Spelling errors also imply that you, or your company, do not proofread and review documents before releasing them. This creates an atmosphere of distrust between the reader and the work instructions. Readers will ignore the work instructions if they feel that the quality is poor.

Grammatical Errors

An instructional step that contains a grammatical error will confuse readers. The reader loses efficiency when they have to re-read a step in the work instruction in an attempt to understand it. The most common cause of this type of error is a sentence fragment which leaves out important details. These errors are dangerous because they lead to incorrectly performed steps.

Missing Steps

A missing step causes major problems with work instructions. Writers often assume that readers have some level of knowledge about the process that the work instruction is explaining. Important details may be omitted that the writer believes are "common knowledge." In reality, readers have a wide variety of backgrounds and skill levels that directly influence their ability to understand instructions. The writer should make an effort to create instructions that will accommodate readers with less-than-expected past experience.

A missing step is a prime suspect when readers must seek help in order to complete the work instructions. Writers must immediately deal with this issue through a document revision to prevent accidents and process errors.

Incorrect Information

Blatantly wrong statements are some of the most dangerous issues in work instructions. The misinformation can easily lead to reader accidents and process errors. This can happen when a process is revised but the work instructions are not updated.

Hidden Information

Information that is hard to find in a work instruction is just as helpful as information that does not exist. Readers will try to figure out the process on their own if they cannot quickly locate what they are searching for in the instructions, and depending on what details the process covers, this can range from a mild inconvenience to a serious issue. The consequences change, depending on what risks the reader exposes themselves to while working. Commonly, the information is difficult to find because navigation sections, such as a table of contents, have been omitted.

Disorganized Collection

When each work instruction in a set is visually or structurally different it can be difficult to navigate through the set. An inconsistent document structure forces the readers to search for specific sections every time they need them. This hassle tends to cause the readers to ignore the instructions all together. This issue is similar to the hidden information issue, but on a larger scope. It normally occurs when there are no style or format guidelines for all work instruction writers in a company to adhere to when creating new documents.

Missed Warnings

Missed warnings are a dangerous subset of hidden information. This situation occurs when readers are not made aware of the dangers associated with certain actions within the work instruction. Besides being potentially dangerous to the reader, it can cause them to distrust the instructions. This situation occurs where there is no standard protocol for formatting and placing warning alerts in documents.

Conclusion

These common issues create a sad state of affairs but are easily fixed with some effort and forethought. Putting in some extra work up-front to create quality documents will avoid countless questions and confusion in the future.

The following sections of this book will hopefully help you overcome these potential failure scenarios and create world class work instructions that people will actually read.

Notes

Chapter 2: Building a Document Framework

The following discussion on document framework, and the subsequent style guide, will form the foundation for all the work instructions that will be created in the future.

What is a framework and why do I need it?

A document framework ensures that all your work instructions are cohesive and follow the same basic layout.

Providing the information in a familiar format helps the reader to quickly learn and understand a new process. Using a familiar framework, the reader will be able to quickly search any work instruction for helpful information. For instance, by using a consistent format, the reader can easily locate the abbreviation list because they know that it is always located right after the Table of Contents.

What does a framework contain?

A document framework can be described as a general outline, or format, to follow when writing work instructions. In a way, a framework can be seen as a work instruction on how to write other work instructions, as it contains general rules about the creation of new documents, including any required sections or information.

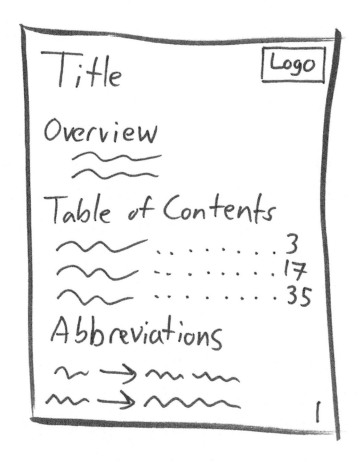

Figure 2: Framework illustration

In general, group the topics logically in the framework so they are easier to find in the completed work instructions. For example, place all lists of figures and tables near the Table of Contents so all the document navigation information is in one area. Another example would be to place the required tools list before each corresponding section if you are writing an assembly focused work instruction.

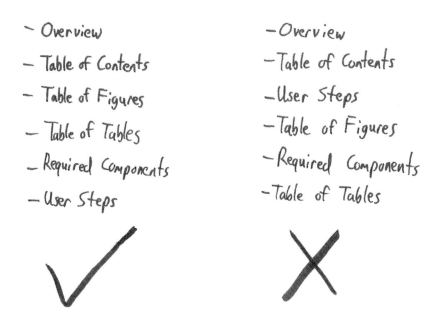

- Overview
- Table of Contents
- Table of Figures
- Table of Tables
- Required Components
- User Steps

- Overview
- Table of Contents
- User Steps
- Table of Figures
- Required Components
- Table of Tables

Figure 3: Grouping topics

The contents of your framework will depend on your own unique circumstance, but the overall goal remains to group the topics in an orderly, sensible manner.

Page Numbers

Make sure to specify that every document includes page numbers. I've seen more documents than I care to admit that have omitted them. The lack of numbering makes it difficult to navigate the document in the best situations and almost impossible to use if the pages get out of order. I always place page numbers in the lower outside corner of the page, making it easy to flip through and find the desired page.

If the page numbers are on the inside or in the middle of the page they are not as readily accessible to the reader.

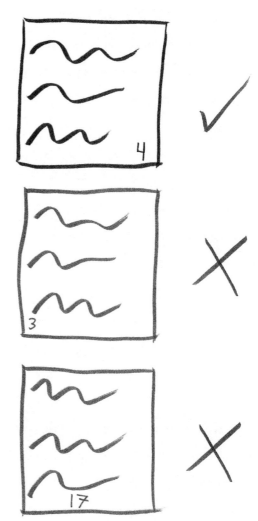

Figure 4: Page number location on right hand page

Attention to small details like page number placement can be the difference between readers using your work instructions effectively, or not at all.

As the number of pages increase, the more the document benefits from proper page number placement.

It is also helpful to have the current page number displayed, along with the total number of pages, to be certain that all the pages are present.

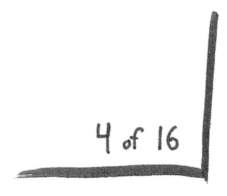

Figure 5: Page number of total

As a final note, if your work instructions will be bound in a booklet with front and back printing, make sure to place them on the lower outside corner of each page. This will require you to alternate the page number location on each page.

Company Logo and Information

Some standard identification information for the work instruction document will be required by your company. This is commonly placed in the document header. Details usually found in the document header include the company logo, contact information, an internal document number, the revision level, and the date of the latest revision.

Initial overview

The initial overview section gives a summary of what the work instruction covers and the target audience.

The main goal of this section is to allow the reader to determine if the document contains the information they seek. In a manufacturing setting, the overview might contain information about the department, personnel level, and the process that is being covered.

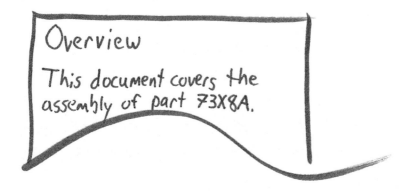

Figure 6: Initial overview

To maximize effectiveness, the initial overview should be placed at the very beginning of a document.

Required Components

I have found that this section is a favorite of work instruction readers. It lists what components are required for the current section of the instructions, or even the entire document.

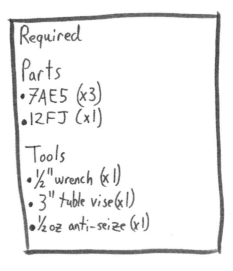

Figure 7: Required components

If there are a large number of required objects, I have found it is beneficial for each section to have its own required components list, so the reader is not overwhelmed by a multipage bulleted list or table.

This practice is common for work instructions in a manufacturing environment where each section lists the inventory parts and the tools required for assembly.

However, sometimes the entire component list should always be in one location, no matter how many entries there are. An ingredient list for a cooking recipe would be an easy example.

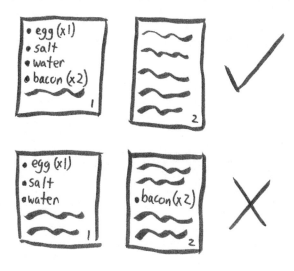

Figure 8: Keep required section together

The readers of the illustrated example will be very unhappy if they get to the second page of this delicious recipe only to find they did not pick up a crucial ingredient when they were at the grocery store. In this case, as well as some others, the entire list of components should be located at the beginning of the instructions because the readers may not be near the required materials and may have to travel some distance to get them.

As the writer of the document, you will have to use your best judgment on how to present the required materials list for each work instruction on an individual basis.

In addition, I have also found that readers appreciate having images of the required items for easier identification. For example, if you have several different sized bolts that are required in one section, it is very handy for the reader to have 1:1 scale images to help determine which bolt is required for each individual step.

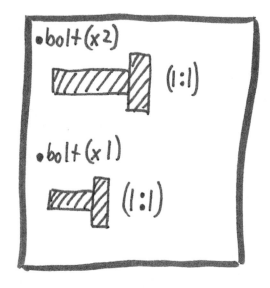

Figure 9: Scale part images 1:1

The reader will be able to hold the part over the work instructions to quickly verify that the bolt is the correct size and length.

In addition to the reader being able to work more efficiently, this approach also reduces the amount of incorrectly installed parts if there are several similar in size or shape.

Table of Contents

A table of contents should be a requirement for almost every document. This helps readers quickly locate desired information within the work instructions. It acts as a barebones summary of the contents if one is not provided in paragraph form. Even short instruction manuals with few sections can benefit from a basic table of contents.

If the work instructions are used as a reference, a table of contents will allow the reader to go directly to what they are looking for without manually skimming the entire document. This can be helpful for experienced readers who have studied the instructions before, but need to refresh on some topics, such as bolt torques, part orientation pictures, optional accessories, or any other information.

List of Abbreviations and their Meanings

A list of abbreviations and their meanings helps clarify any abbreviations that are used in the work instructions. Every abbreviation used should be explained as each reader may have a different idea of what it could mean.

The lack of a list of abbreviations and meanings is one of the most common problems I find when reading work instructions. The document writer assumes that the reader knows certain organizational or field-specific jargon, when in reality, they rarely know this information beforehand.

List of Figures

This list shows the title of any figures and their corresponding page number within the document. It allows readers to find the helpful images that have been included in your work instruction. This section becomes more important, and is used more often by the reader, as the quality of images in the work instruction improve.

List of Tables

This list shows the title of any tables and their corresponding page number in the work instruction. The list helps the readers find crucial information within the document that you have tabulated.

Referenced Form List

This list indicates any forms that must be filled out when working through this particular set of instructions. For example, the reader may have to fill out a form to record specific information about what they are building, such as part serial numbers or other traceable identification information. This section will make sure that the readers gather all the additional paperwork before beginning the work instruction.

External Document References

This list details documents such as international standards, a company quality manual, or any other type of external document referenced in the work instructions. Normally documents in this list are not needed for following the work instructions, but serve as references for quality system requirements, or to indicate where some referenced information originated.

Troubleshooting

A troubleshooting section shows common issues with the process and ways to fix those problems. This section is commonly included in documents that will be seen and used by customers or other readers who deal with complex machinery. There are several formats that this section could take, including but not limited to: numbered steps, flowcharts, and tables.

Figure 10: Troubleshooting with steps

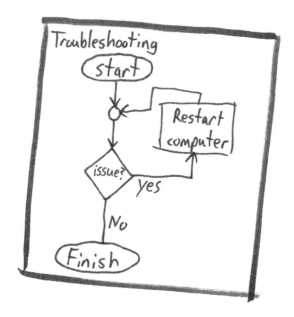

Figure 11: Troubleshooting with a flowchart

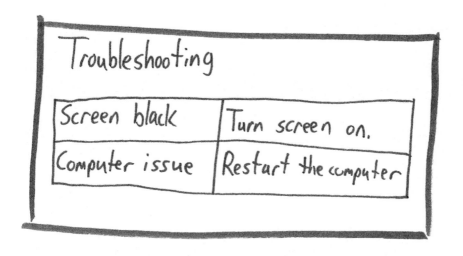

Figure 12: Troubleshooting with a table

Revision Table

A revision table shows a brief history of the minor changes to the document since its initial release. It is most often used for internal documents in between major revisions. A major revision is a substantial edit that would take too much explaining to fit into a revision table. Documents provided to customers or other external personnel usually do not include this section.

I do not normally include a revision table as part of a work instruction because it is seldom used by the reader. If revision information is needed, there should be some quality software in use that tracks document revisions or holds archival copies of the previous versions.

In Conclusion

You will need to determine what sections will be required for your work instructions in order for them to be as useful as possible for your audience. Some of these choices will be obvious, like a Table of Contents, and others will have to be added over time as you receive feedback from your readers.

It is common to have multiple frameworks to use for different types of work instructions. A work instruction that covers product assembly will differ in structure from one which covers equipment operation and should have its own framework.

Example Framework

I have created a simple framework to illustrate what one of these documents might look like. The one shown below would be used in a manufacturing environment to explain the process of assembling some type of equipment or product.

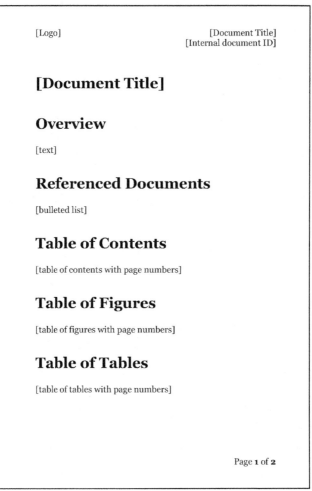

Figure 13: Example framework page 1

[Logo]

[Document Title]
[Internal document ID]

Required Components

[bulleted list or table of required parts and tools]

Assembly Steps

[multi-level steps]

Page **2** of **2**

Figure 14: Example framework page 2

Notes

Chapter 3: Crafting a Style Guide

Creating a style guide and using the framework that you have developed complete the foundation for all your upcoming work instructions.

What is a style guide and why do I need it?

A style guide's purpose is to keep all document formatting similar, and it also conveys the appropriate level of caution when needed. The style guide can drive you, and even an entire department of writers, toward common themes and warning symbols that are familiar and easily recognizable by readers.

What does a style guide contain?

A style guide can be seen as the recipe for how all new work instructions should look. It will contain general rules about the different types of text and the use of corresponding font formatting. The contents of your style guide will depend on your unique circumstances, but here are some sections to get you started:

[Handwritten annotations: Headings Bold; Left Align; Calibri 12 is Body; 1.5; Headings 16pt]

Font Choice

Having a defined font for use in every document will help ensure that all work instructions will be easily readable. Having a defined font avoids the selection of any artistic fonts that can detract from the readability of the document. Your defined font can be any font that you choose, but I recommend choosing one of the standard serif fonts that your word processing software has available. These fonts have small lines on the letters that help guide the reader's eyes across the page.

It is generally accepted that serif fonts are easier to read than sans serif fonts; and readability is an important factor for technical documents such as work instructions.

Font Size

Font sizes will vary depending on what type of text is being written and in what manner the text will be used in the document. For example, document titles and paragraph headers should be larger in size than the body font. Also, all text used on an instructional poster should be larger than the test used in a typical book-style work instruction.

I recommend that body text be at least 12pt. Each level of headings should increase by two or four points, enabling

[Handwritten annotation: Paragraph spacing]

readers to quickly differentiate between the headlines at a glance.

Font Effects

It is important to specify what font effects will be allowed in different styles of text. In general, font effects should only be used to make an impactful difference, otherwise you risk having the document appear messy and overdone.

Bold

One section of the guide should specify what headings are to be bold and which headings are to remain regular type.

Italics

The style guide should specify that italics are not allowed for normal text because italics make reading text more difficult.

Underline

Underlining normal text should be avoided, because in the modern age most people associate underlined words with hyperlinks. Underlining can be confusing if readers are viewing a digital copy of the work instructions.

Line Spacing

When determining the spacing between the lines of the body font, I recommend around one-and-a-half lines of space. Single spaced lines tend to appear crowded to readers, and double-spaced lines leave excessive room that is only useful for adding manual corrections to a document.

Single Spacing

This text has single line spacing. It looks cramped on the page, which will lower readability.

One-and-a-Half Spacing

This text has one-and-a-half line spacing. This book also uses one-and-a-half line spacing throughout. I believe that it provides the best balance between readability and conserving space.

Double Spacing

This text has double line spacing. Double spacing provides an excessive amount of white space between the lines. Double spacing is helpful when a document in a draft stage will be manually marked-up because the editor will have sufficient room to write corrections.

Paragraph Spacing

Now let's move on to paragraph spacing which is the spacing before and after paragraphs and other styles of text.

You should never use the enter key to insert spaces between any type of text.

Figure 15: No enter key

Instead, set up the spacing within the text style in your software to control the paragraph spacing automatically. This will keep the text spacing uniform throughout the instructions with no effort on your part.

In regard to general spacing, you should space headings so that they are closer to the text they represent, rather than the text they follow. Just a few extra points of spacing will produce noticeable results, which helps visually group the sections of text and improve readability.

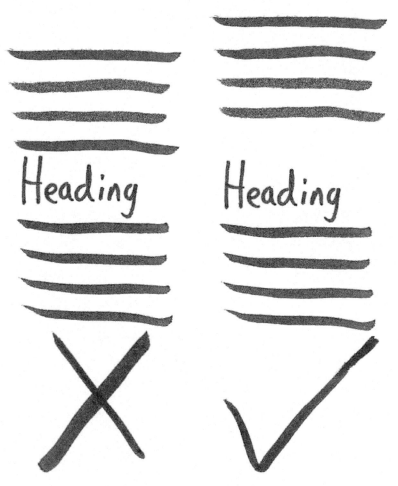

Figure 16: Paragraph spacing

Text Alignment

The consistent alignment of the document's text is an often-overlooked aspect of easy readability. Let's look at the different styles.

Left Align

This paragraph is left aligned. This is the appropriate format for work instructions. The jagged end points of each line allow the reader to more easily pick back up where they left off after looking away to perform an indicated action.

Justified

This paragraph is justified. This is the not the appropriate format for work instructions because the common endpoint on each line of justified text makes it harder for the user to remember where they left off when reading. This blob of text lowers the reader's efficiency due to the inability to find their previous stopping point.

Right Align

This paragraph is right aligned. This is not appropriate for work instructions that use languages that read left to right. Right alignment can be used for text in special situations but is generally not used when creating work instructions.

Page Setup

The general page properties can also be specified in your style guide. These can include paper size, page orientation, and margins.

These settings are normally specified to ensure that all printed documents are able to be placed into binders and aligned with other documents. This can be especially crucial for external documents that might be bound together to give to customers or other outside personnel. It is important that all the pages stack uniformly on one another and their margins be adequate for installing into a ring binder without interfering with any content.

Perspective

The viewpoint of work instructions should almost always be in third person. This gives the documents a more professional look and improves the overall quality of the instructions. The document should not read like someone else is telling them personally how to follow the work instruction, but as if they are looking over someone else's shoulder and copying every action.

Table Formatting

Formatting a table should be carefully considered, because tables can become unreadable and unhelpful very quickly. I suggest the following guidelines for any tables that make their way into your instructions:

Keep the header text simple and minimally formatted. I suggest you leave the font size and alignment exactly the same as the rest of that column, but simply make this text bold to differentiate it.

Table 1: Table header example

Column Header 1	Column Header 2
Data0	Data2
Data1	Data3

Every other row should have a light gray background to improve readability across multiple columns. However, make sure the shading is very light or it can mask the data. The shading tactic is especially helpful when dealing with tables that have many columns, as it is easy to lose your row when scanning across the page if the rows are all the same.

Table 2: Table row shading example

Column Header 1	Column Header 2
Data0	Data2
Data1	Data3

All columns with text, or mixed text and numbers, should be left-aligned. All columns with numbers only should be right-aligned. The reasoning behind right alignment for numbers is to line up the decimal places for easier comparison and analysis.

Table 3: Table text versus number formatting

Description Column	Value Column
This stuff	$104.67
Those things	$18.93

I caution you against using a variety of formatting techniques within a single table as the table will become unreadable and confusing very quickly. Simple techniques are the most effective when trying to communicate tabulated information to the readers.

When setting column widths, allow some extra room around the values in the table. This "white space" will make the table easier to read and more visually appealing, because it will not appear crowded.

Attention Grabbers

Attention grabbers are generally small pieces of information indirectly tied to a process or a particular step. Attention grabbers include things like informational notes, as well as caution, warning, and danger alerts.

Figure 17: Example attention grabber

Every attention grabber should consist of a standardized symbol, followed by the corresponding text. Be aware; if a variety of symbols are used for a single category, readers may not know at a glance what the various symbols mean, and may be more likely to skip over the important text.

Using a common icon and format for each type of attention grabber will help readers associate a visual cue with a certain level of risk. For example, every time the reader comes across the exclamation point symbol, they will know that the next step presents some level of risk, and they will have to act in a more careful manner.

Other formatting options for attention grabbers, such as increasing the font size or applying bold to the text, can be used to add additional emphasis if desired. However, do not rely on warning colors, such as red, to alert readers because this effect will be lost if the document is printed in black and white. In my experience, almost all documents printed for use by shop personnel end up being printed in black and white.

The following caution text is easily recognized because the font size is larger than the surrounding body text and has the bold effect. It is easily noticeable on a computer screen and on a printed document.

Caution! Wear safety glasses.

The next example of a caution text relies on the color red to indicate danger. It looks really good on the computer screen, but when printed in black and white and sent to the work area, you can see that the emphasis is lost.

Caution! Wear safety glasses.

This issue could potentially cause the reader to overlook a crucial safety step, and it should be avoided.

All attention grabbers should precede its corresponding step. This is especially important for dangers, warnings, and cautions, because harm could come to the reader if they do not abide by the attention grabber.

This may seem obvious but, in my experience, I have come across documents where necessary safety information was hidden within a step or placed afterward.

In order to handle how each type of attention grabber is used, I add a risk section to the work instructions that I write. This section defines what each attention grabber symbol means and the level of associated risk. The following examples are similar to those I include while writing my own work instructions:

Risk 0 of 3: Information
This note indicates tasks that pose no risk to the reader or the current process they are working on.

Figure 18: Information attention grabber

The content of this type of message is purely informational, such as helpful tips on how to complete a step more easily.

Risk 1 of 3: Caution

This note indicates tasks that pose a low level of risk to the reader, the current process, or both.

Figure 19: Caution attention grabber

The content of this type of message should indicate what the risk is and how to properly address the situation. These notes are used regularly and can indicate things such as minor cuts from handling sharp parts, or a bolt that is commonly cross-threaded in the part.

Risk 2 of 3: Warning

This note indicates tasks that pose a moderate to high level of risk to the reader, the current process, or both.

Figure 20: Warning attention grabber

The content of this type of message should indicate what the risk is and how to properly handle the situation. These notes are used semi-regularly and can indicate things such as pinch points, making sure to relieve any residual low pressure from a system before beginning work, or ensuring that oil is added to equipment before attempting to start it for the first time.

Risk 3 of 3: Danger

This note indicates a task that poses an extreme level of risk to the reader.

Figure 21: Danger attention grabber

The content of this type of message should clearly state exactly what the risk is and how to properly manage it. The message should be very detailed and cover all the required protection measures and safety equipment necessary to keep the reader safe.

These notes should be used sparingly so the reader will take the note seriously when present in the text.

The types of risks that danger messages cover include grievous bodily harm or death. As an example, this level of attention grabber should be used in situations that include possible loss of extremities, risk of electrocution, or possible exposure to toxic gases.

General Notes

Make sure to go over the risk levels in your work instruction with your onsite safety manager to properly indicate all levels of risk that you need to address. The safety manager may have an existing set of attention grabber symbols that you should use to express risk in a way that is already familiar to the readers.

In Conclusion

The style guide will prove to be a valuable resource for ensuring that all work instructions maintain the desired level of polish and clarity. I have found that it is very helpful to save presets into your word processing software so that everyone is automatically using the desired style settings. As with the rest of these documents discussed, your style guide can, and probably should, differ from the sample one that we are about to review so that your style guide meets your unique goals.

Example Style Guide

I have created a simple style guide to illustrate an example of one of these documents. This one is remarkably similar to how this book is formatted.

[Logo]

Style Guide
[Internal document ID]

Work Instructions Style Guide

This document will outline the proper formatting for creating new work instructions.

Table of Contents

Page **1** of **8**

Figure 22: Example style guide page 1

[Logo]

Style Guide
[Internal document ID]

General Notes

All documents should adhere to the following guidelines:

1. All line spacing should be set at "1.5 lines."
2. Italics are not to be used.
3. Underline is only to be used for hyperlinks in documents that will be viewed on an electronic device.
4. All text should be left aligned.
5. All documents should be written in third person perspective.
6. Do not use the Enter key to add spaces to the document.

Font Styles

This section will detail what settings should be used for various types of text.

Heading 1

- Font: Georgia
- Font Size: 20 pt.

Page **2** of **8**

Figure 23: Example style guide page 2

[Logo]

Style Guide
[Internal document ID]

- Font Effect: Bold
- Spacing, Before: 20 pt.
- Spacing, After: 6 pt.

Heading 2

- Font: Georgia
- Font Size: 16 pt.
- Font Effect: Bold
- Spacing, Before: 18 pt.
- Spacing, After: 6 pt.

Heading 3

- Font: Georgia
- Font Size: 16 pt.
- Font Effect: None
- Spacing, Before: 18 pt.
- Spacing, After: 6 pt.

Page **3** of **8**

Figure 24: Example style guide page 3

[Logo]

Style Guide
[Internal document ID]

Heading 4

- Font: Georgia
- Font Size: 12 pt.
- Font Effect: Bold
- Spacing, Before: 18 pt.
- Spacing, After: 6 pt.

Normal

- Font: Georgia
- Font Size: 12 pt.
- Font Effect: None
- Spacing, Before: 0 pt.
- Spacing, After: 8 pt.

Step Formatting

- Use Normal text style.
- Use numerical multi-level lists.
- Steps in appendices or other special sections should be preceded by an identifying letter.

Page **4** of **8**

Figure 25: Example style guide page 4

[Logo] Style Guide
[Internal document ID]

- Example for Appendix A: step A3.4

Table Formatting

- Use Normal text style.
- Color every other row a very light shade of gray.
- All columns with text should be left aligned.
- All columns with numbers should be right aligned.

Attention Grabbers

- Font: Georgia
- Font Size: 16 pt.
- Font Effect: None
- Spacing, Before: 0 pt.
- Spacing, After: 8 pt.
- Preceded by the appropriate standard symbol for the risk level associated with the action being performed.

Risk 0 of 3: Information

This note indicates tasks that pose no risk to the reader or the current process they are working on.

Page **5** of **8**

Figure 26: Example style guide page 5

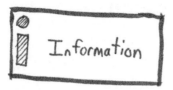

Figure 1: Information attention grabber

The content of this type of message is purely informational, such as helpful tips on how to complete a step more easily.

Risk 1 of 3: Caution

This note indicates tasks that pose a low level of risk to the reader, the current process, or both.

Figure 2: Caution attention grabber

The content of this type of message should indicate what the risk is and how to properly address the situation. These notes are used regularly and can indicate things such as minor cuts from handling sharp parts, or a bolt that is commonly cross-threaded in the part.

Figure 27: Example style guide page 6

Risk 2 of 3: Warning

This note indicates tasks that pose a moderate to high level of risk to the reader, the current process, or both.

Figure 3: Warning attention grabber

The content of this type of message should indicate what the risk is and how to properly handle the situation. These notes are used semi-regularly and can indicate things such as pinch points, making sure to relieve any residual low pressure from a system before beginning work, or ensuring that oil is added to equipment before attempting to start it for the first time.

Risk 3 of 3: Danger

This note indicates a task that poses an extreme level of risk to the reader.

Figure 28: Example style guide page 7

Figure 4: Danger attention grabber

The content of this type of message should clearly state exactly what the risk is and how to properly manage it. The message should be very detailed and cover all the required protection measures and safety equipment necessary to keep the reader safe.

These notes should be used sparingly so the reader will take the note seriously when present in the text.

The types of risks that danger messages cover include grievous bodily harm or death. As an example, this level of attention grabber should be used in situations that include possible loss of extremities, risk of electrocution, or possible exposure to toxic gases.

Figure 29: Example style guide page 8

Notes

Chapter 4: Writing Superior Steps

Now that we have created a solid foundation for our work instructions we can move on to the most important part, the individual steps of the work instructions. These steps are the core of the document and should be carefully constructed to maximize their impact on the reader. Here are a few things to keep in mind while writing:

Number Every Single Step

Each step should be sequentially numbered in a multi-level list format for ease of identifying which step a reader is currently acting on. A simple example of this format follows.

1. Level one

    1.1. Level two

    1.1.1.Level three

2. Level one continued

Numbering steps has a dramatic effect on steps that are accidentally skipped by the reader. It also improves the document experience for the reader because the numbering system helps them to find their place in the instructions after they have performed the current action.

The numbering should start over for appendices or other sections that are separate from the main text and could include the appendix identifier as the first digit.

Main Document Steps

1. Do this.

2. Do that.

    2.1. More on how to do that.

3. Done.

Appendix Steps

A1. Look at this.

A2.Look at that.

    A2.1. More on how to look at that.

A3.Done.

This helps to prevent the instructions from causing confusion by having multiple "step 2.1"'s and other similar situations.

One Action per Step

Limit each step of the work instruction to a single action. Single tasks make instructions easier to follow and comprehend. I have found that multiple tasks within one step this is the most common root cause of reader error while following a work instruction.

Readers who are be skimming the instructions are likely to only look at the first part of the step before moving on to the next one. If multiple actions are included in a single numbered step, there is an increased likelihood that readers will skip an action.

The one exception to the single action per step rule is if the reader must perform multiple actions simultaneously. This can occur when the actions are fundamentally interlinked, or the reader would have to redo the previous step in order to easily complete the current one. Let's take a look at a sample set of instructions for submitting a printed document to see this in action.

1. Stack all of the papers. Take care to align the edges. Staple all of the papers together.

2. Place in the submission box.

This work instruction is poorly written because there are multiple actions within a single numbered step. This can lead to readers skipping over steps and causing process errors. You would be surprised how many readers would skip stapling the papers together before submitting them in the submission box.

Now let's go over a slightly modified version of the previous instructions.

1. Taking care to align the edges, stack all of the papers.

2. Staple all of the papers together.

3. Place the papers into the submission box.

This updated version of the work instruction is much improved. Each step has one main action, with the exception of the first step. The first step showcases the exception to the single action rule because the reader has to align all of the pages at the same time as they stack them. In the updated version, there should be no reason for a reader to miss a step or cause any errors in the process, such as neglecting to staple all of the papers together before submitting them.

Be Concise

Another important part of writing effective action steps is keeping the steps concise. A surprisingly large number of people do not read the entire step before moving on to the next one when the steps are viewed as unhelpful or wordy.

However, be careful to avoid steps that are too bare-boned. Make sure your steps are written in a sentence format to improve readability.

Let's take a look at some examples of steps to illustrate this point.

Not enough words

1. Lay out parts.

2. Inspect for dings, other damage.

Too many words

1. Lay all of the small parts, medium parts, and large parts onto a flat, table-like surface that has adequate room to accommodate every single one of the parts with some space to spare.

2. Inspect the small parts, the medium parts, and the large parts for tiny hard-to-see dings, as well as humongous obvious dings, and other damage that can be noticed by

the naked human eye without any special observation equipment.

Just the right amount of words

1. Lay all of the parts onto a flat surface.

2. Inspect the parts for dings and other damage.

Hopefully you noticed that the third set of instructions in an effective balance between easy readability and minimal step length. The goal is to give the reader exactly as much information as they need to easily complete a step, but not so much as to discourage them from reading through the entire action. Paying attention to these small details goes a long way in creating a positive reader experience and outcome.

Every step should be explained in a clear manner to prevent the reader from having to infer or guess at what they are supposed to be doing. We can see this more clearly with an example.

Consider the actions required to install a round cover onto a flange with threaded holes.

1. Place the gasket onto the flange face.

2. Taking care to align the bolt holes, lay the cover on top of the gasket.

3. Thread the bolts through the cover into the threaded flange holes.

4. Torque the flange bolts to 150 ft-lbs.

The torque pattern that is needed to ensure a consistent seal may not be apparent to some readers, depending upon their previous experience and training. Make sure that everything in the step is clearly defined to ensure consistent results from everyone who follows the instructions. If the reader has to infer how to perform a process in a step, then inconsistencies will occur.

An improved version of the previous instructions follows.

1. Place the gasket onto the flange face.

2. Taking care to align the bolt holes, lay the cover on top of the gasket.

3. Thread the bolts through the cover into the threaded flange holes.

4. Torque the flange bolts to 150 ft-lbs in three equal steps of 50 ft-lbs, using a star pattern.

These actions are much clearer than the original and should help readers successfully complete the process.

Include All Relevant Steps

On a related note, what is considered to be a simple step is highly subjective, so be sure to include all steps, no matter how insignificant the steps may seem to you. There are some obviously extreme instances of this that you should avoid, but in general it is better to give more explanation than is necessary, rather than not enough.

When writing instructions for software processes, I include a step for every button click and dealing with every prompt. This way, the instructions are helpful for everyone, no matter how computer literate they may or may not be. The more advanced users use these instructions for specific functions that they use irregularly, while the beginner users use them verbatim to perform a wide variety of tasks.

In the end, you will learn to fine tune the steps of each of your work instructions to be effective for each unique audience.

Including Images Where Appropriate

Great work instructions include images wherever it is appropriate. A good rule of thumb is that if you have to think about how to explain a step, then it needs an image to help clarify the process for the reader.

Placing good quality images in your work instructions will yield the greatest increase in reader satisfaction than any other method. A single well-placed image has the capability to clarify or oven replace paragraphs of detailed steps. This clarity will lower the number of workplace errors that occur from readers misunderstanding the work instruction.

For instance, the steps from the previous example could be improved even further by including an image.

1. Place the gasket onto the flange face.

2. Taking care to align the bolt holes, lay the cover on top of the gasket.

3. Thread the bolts through the cover into the threaded flange holes.

4. Torque the flange bolts to 150 ft-lbs in three equal steps of 50 ft-lbs, using a star pattern as shown.

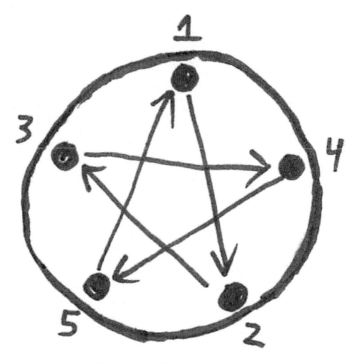

Figure 30: Torque pattern

This image indicates exactly what torque pattern is desired by the writer and leaves nothing to the reader's interpretation.

Images can be either hand-drawn or created with the help of computer software. Each style has its own share of benefits that are appropriate for different types of work instructions. For work instructions that are used in a manufacturing environment, I recommend that you utilize some sort of software when creating the images. If your work instruction is a culinary recipe or some other creative process, then hand-drawn illustrations can add some charm, while still providing helpful information, to the document.

Image Location and Format

It is nice to have an overview drawing at the beginning of each work instruction section in order to provide a brief summary of what will be covered. This could be an exploded view of the assembly covered in this section, or a screenshot of the application window that the reader will be using.

Images should be located as close as possible to the steps that reference them. If the image is in sight along with the corresponding step, then it is generally acceptable. I have found that if the images are placed on the next page, readers will not look at the images until it is too late.

When formatting images, try to create them so they will be clear when printed in black and white. Documents that are meant for use by shop personnel are almost always printed in grayscale, and the images can be unreadable if the originals are in color. Wireframe images that only indicate the outline are the best option, as they look good when viewed on monitors and when printed in any color scheme.

As a final note, all images should have a caption below them for reference, whether or not you have included a Table of Figures in the document.

In Conclusion

The individual steps of a work instruction form the core material, and these steps have the largest impact on the overall quality of the document. Creating a well-written set of steps will clear one major hurdle on the way to making readers actually want to follow your instructions.

Notes

Chapter 5: Helpful Tips

Let's discuss some of the helpful tidbits that I have gathered from writing my own work instructions and other technical documents.

Seek Feedback

So, you have your great new work instruction written and ready. Now the only issue is getting people to read your instructions in the first place.

One tactic I have found to be very successful is to ask your target audience to read through your work instructions and ask them what could be improved. Asking the readers for their opinions on the documents motivates them to carefully read through the entirety of the work instructions. This review process will give readers their first impression of the work instructions, so be sure to make a good impact. The better first impression the reader has, the more likely they will use your work instructions in the future.

By having the target audience read the work instructions, you often get useful feedback about the ordering of steps, or what sections seem confusing and need improvement. Experienced readers will also be able to tell you about easier methods to accomplish the desired actions. There is no substitute for experience, and your readers are one of the best sources to tap into for improving your work instructions.

In addition, observing people work through your instructions for the first time is an enlightening process that will help you determine where the readers need additional information. Any step which they repeatedly refer back to is a step that needs some improvement. This can be accomplished through a number of methods, such as rewording the step or adding a clarifying illustration.

Overall, it is important to remember that your documents can always be improved, and reader feedback is a very direct way of finding out what works and what doesn't.

Print One-Sided

One-sided printing ensures that the reader does not have to deal with blurry text because of bleed through from the back side of the page. If blurriness is present, it can make a work instruction seem to be of poor quality, even when it is well written. Single-sided prints are also easier to flip through, because you do not have to continually flip the pages over as you go through the document.

Do Not Link Steps to One Another by Number

Do not reference other steps by manually typing the number because if steps are added or removed in future revisions, the numbers will no longer match up, causing confusion. It is also a great hassle to search through the instructions to find and update the referenced step numbers every time a change is made.

Before Revision

1. Do this.

2. Do something else.

    2.1. If this happens then repeat step 2.

3. Finally do this.

After Revision

1. Do this.

2. Newly added thing to do.

3. Do something else.

    3.1. If this happens then repeat step 2.

4. Finally do this.

If your word processing software has a cross-reference feature it can be used to automatically update step numbers and avoid reader confusion. Using a software feature similar to this is the only way that I would recommend for linking steps by their number.

Proofread Everything

Have someone who was not involved with writing the document proofread it. A fresh set of eyes will often be able to immediately pick out the small errors that have been overlooked.

Figure 31: Always proofread

Proofreading is especially critical if the document is going to be released to customers or the general public. It is easier and more cost effective to catch errors before the documents are printed in bulk for distribution. It is much more than just embarrassing and unprofessional to have obvious errors — I have seen printed documents worth tens of thousands of dollars thrown away because of obvious typos and errors that would have been caught with proofreading.

Always Include Units

You should always specify the units for numerical values. Never assume that the reader will know which units are implied. A work instruction could be read in a locale that was not originally expected, where the local "standard" units differ from the original intent.

Furthermore, omitting the specific units can lead to potentially catastrophic situations. For example, there is a meaningful difference between 150 psi and 150 bar of pressure. However, if the work instruction reads "Pressure up the system to 150," the readers will not know what that sentence means if there are no associated units stated.

Even in situations where the result would not be harmful, unit-less numbers lead to reader confusion and the need for unnecessary clarification.

Always include units.

Adapt

The framework and style guide can, and should, change over time as you receive more feedback from your readers. In order to create the best experience for your readers, you will have to update the format and structure periodically to include improvements and to appeal to new audiences.

Make Use of Built-In Functionality

Make use of built-in software functions, such as automatic tables of contents, figures, tables, and references in order to save time creating new documents.

Any time saving measures will make it that much easier for you to adhere to the style guidelines.

Assign Forms to Critical Steps

Vital steps may have an accompanying form or checklist to help ensure compliance. These forms should be included in the "Referenced Form" list that you have specified in your framework.

White Space

One of the largest contributors to document readability is the proper use of "white space." Sometimes the best thing to include in an area is nothing at all. White space helps separate each section and visually guides the reader through the document. For the best reader experience, their eyes need to flow smoothly through the instructions.

For instance, instead of squeezing in helpful notes next to every step, you could place them before the step. This simple change will reduce how crowded the work instructions feel while reading.

Notes

Chapter 6: Conclusion

Now that you have a basic overview of how to write great work instructions that people will actually read, let's briefly revisit some of the key points.

Most work instructions fail to meet the very basic criteria of being well written and the readers end up with questions and doubts while working through the document. These poorly written documents prevent the reader from being able to go through the entire work instruction process and achieve the desired results. Now that you understand why most work instructions fail, you can actively avoid writing instructions that fall into this dire category.

The document framework gives us all of the required sections that any work instruction must have and keeps the sections in a familiar format. The document framework provides a standard template that ensures the readers' experience will be consistent throughout a related set of work instructions.

The style guide keeps the work instructions consistent by providing a set of rules to govern how each document must look, criteria for any attention grabbers you might use, and how images should be formatted within the document. The style guide ensures that all the work instructions form a cohesive collection and all important information is easily recognized by the reader.

The basic rule for writing solid work instruction steps is to concisely inform the reader of the required actions. Solid action steps guide the reader easily and efficiently through learning a process and have the most direct impact on the reader's opinion of the work instructions.

All of these topics combined create a solid foundation upon which you can create a collection of work instructions that are helpful and cohesive.

I hope that this book has prepared you for success in creating work instructions that people actually want to read.

Good luck out there. —Kyle

About the Author

Kyle Shropshire is a mechanical engineer, programmer, and automation enthusiast. Somehow, he has found time to begin sharing his experiences from his engineering career, as well as his hobbies, in between working and running a CNC mill on his coffee table.

Printed in Great Britain
by Amazon